Primer for
CHRISTIAN MEDITATION

Robert F. Willett
CSC

MOREHOUSE-BARLOW COMPANY
Wilton, Connecticut

© 1976 Morehouse-Barlow Co., Inc.
Wilton, Connecticut

Standard Book Number 0-8192-1202-4

Printed in the United States
of America

TABLE OF CONTENTS

Page

Introduction 4

Section One — MEDITATION 5
   On Meditation 7

Section Two — NEW PRAYER FORMS . . . 25
   Private Vocal Prayer 28
   Communal Vocal Prayer 41
   Group Meditation 44
   A Concluding Word on Prayer 60

INTRODUCTION

Another prayer study? Yes! Even though many already exist, there's always room for one more because prayer is so central to the life of man with God. There are many books and articles written about the theories and formulas for prayer. The purpose of this book is to explain *how* to pray — a manual of practice.

The first section is devoted to meditation, explained step-by-step in the simplest language possible. This method is simpler than those of St. Ignatius, St. Francis de Sales, or the Sulpician method, among others. It is suitable for beginners and has enough substance for one who has meditated long, and perhaps with difficulty, according to one of the more traditional methods. I have placed the meditation section first because the practice of meditation has the power to deepen insights and strengthen the will thus giving meaning to other kinds of prayer. Meditation needs stressing because it has been much neglected in Western spirituality in recent centuries, relegated to monasteries, priests, and religious when it should be a prayer form for every Christian.

The second part is devoted to new methods of private and communal vocal prayer. No doubt the list of new forms could be expanded, but enough examples are given to enable the reader to choose the best personal forms.

In all things I have tried to write in the simplest form possible with as little philosophizing and theologizing as possible. In truth I desired to make a handbook for actual practice. Those who wish to know more of the theory are urged to read books on prayer. The best course of action, however, is to start praying.

Robert F. Willett
CSC

SECTION ONE

MEDITATION

MEDITATION

On Meditation

Today people are hungry for prayer, yet many are finding it harder and harder to pray. Prayer should be as simple as breathing, as natural as eating, drinking, and sleeping. It is simply relating ourselves to God, and human nature cries out for such a relation.

Today it is no longer considered "kooky" to be interested in forms of Eastern mysticism such as Zen and Yoga, and a large number of people, especially young people, are caught up in transcendental meditation. Hence I needn't hesitate to state that this method is largely based on Zen. Even Thomas Merton recognized that the East had millenia of experience in the practice of meditation, while we of the West have largely neglected it.

Forms of prayer can be classified as liturgical, communal-vocal, private-vocal, and meditation. Of these forms it is meditation that has the power to change our lives and conform us to God, yet it is most neglected today. When we are told that we must pray more we immediately think of multiplying vocal prayer, either communally or privately. Members of religious congregations find less time to meditate and more difficulty in its practice. Perhaps this is due to the cumbersome methods of St. Ignatius with which they have never been able to be comfortable. Meditation should be pleasant. If practiced properly, it can answer a basic need of our being. The method I shall describe can restore joy, spontaneity, and the longing to enter into a relationship with God. This method is based on Zen, but I won't use Zen words, recommend difficult exercises or uncomfortable positions, and avoid all philosophical discussions and explanations. If the reader wishes to learn more about these things the bibliography at the end of the section provides some excellent references.

Place and Time

Choose a quiet place. Human noises are very distracting, but natural sounds, such as wind or water may be soothing. A room neither too dark nor too light, neither

too warm nor too cold is preferable. If there is an error it should be on the side of coolness. Choose a time of day when you are alert and when you have time, quiet, and solitude. A good length of time for beginners to allot themselves is thirty minutes, but fifteen minutes is better than nothing. Regular daily practice of meditative prayer is necessary if progress in intimacy with God is to be achieved.

Bodily Position for Meditation

Manuals on meditation written for Western Christians don't make much of bodily positions, whereas all Eastern mysticisms stress that the position of the body has much to do with the success of the meditation. Without giving a long explanation I will say I believe the East is more correct. Body and soul form a unity. The body must also be redeemed and must pray. I will recommend three positions.

The first position is the seated posture. Use a straight-backed chair, but don't lean against the back of the chair. The feet should rest firmly on the floor. What is more important is that the spinal column be straight. All Eastern masters stress that a lapse in concentration can be recognized by the slumping of the back. The head should be erect, looking straight ahead, the ears in line with the shoulders, the tip of the nose approximately in line with the navel. During meditation occasionally check your posture, especially if you find yourself losing concentration.

The second position is achieved by kneeling, the toes pointed away from the body, extending straight backwards. Place a pillow on the heels and sit back so that you are sitting on your heels and calves. The position of the upper body should be the same as described above, the spinal column straight.

The third position is the one used by Eastern masters and monks: the lotus position. It is usually painful to maintain for long periods and the pain disappears only after much practice. Begin this position by sitting on the floor on a cushion. Place your right foot on your left thigh, and then place your left foot on your right thigh. Bring your knees into contact with the floor. This gives you a solid base of great stability and immobility.

Experiment with these positions and choose the one that best lends itself to concentration and meditation.

After assuming your bodily position, place your right hand in your lap, palm upward. Then place the left hand, also palm upward, on top of the right. Bring the tips of the thumbs together lightly so that the two hands form a shallow oval.

In this steady position, your meditation won't be disturbed by bodily movements; concentration is jarred by any movement. One who has meditated in the presence of others has seen slouching and leaning bodies in all sorts of undisciplined postures, accompanied by constant shifts of position. After seeing such meditation positions one cannot help feeling assured by the solidity of any of the three positions described above, and will surely experience how they set his mind free for its work. A final reminder, for it cannot be repeated too often: make sure the spine is straight!

Eyes

Keep the eyes open. If the eyes close the mind easily wanders. Lower the gaze slightly so that the eyes are about half open. The position of the head should not be changed. Let your gaze be unfocused, not concentrating on any one object. Perhaps you might find it helpful to place a crucifix six to eight feet from you, resting it either on the floor or against a wall. I would recommend that you first try meditating without this aid, and use it only if necessary.

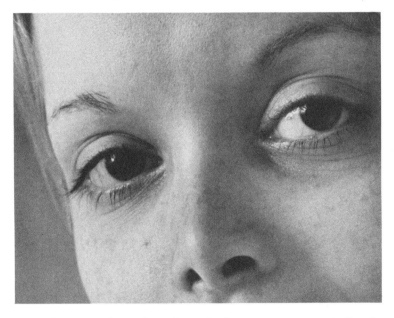

To begin, take a deep breath, letting it out noiselessly through the nose. Perhaps as a beginner you might take two or three of these breaths, but later one should be sufficient.

First Meditation

After your deep breath begin breathing normally and rhythmically. To pray to God you must first be present to yourself — if you aren't present to yourself you can't be present to God. The first part of this meditation is intended to make you present to yourself.

Silently count "one" as you inhale, and "two" as you exhale. Continue counting up to ten, and then return to "one." Concentrate on the number as you count. Count breaths for perhaps five series of ten. or until you find yourself keeping count easily. If you find this being present to yourself pleasant, don't hesitate to extend the counting of breaths.

My method is both eclectic and personal. The next recommendation reflects another source. Counting breaths makes you present to yourself. Now you must become present to God. To do this I have used the Jesus Prayer. This form of prayer arose in Russia and was meant to become so much a mental and physical habit that it became constant, a current underlying working, eating, talking, even sleeping. It becomes constant because it is synchronized with breathing rhythms. Recite the prayer silently "Lord Jesus Christ, Son of God," as the breath is drawn in, and then "have mercy on me a sinner" as the breath is exhaled. When this is practiced assiduously it becomes a continual prayer the person is aware of even in the midst of absorbing activities. I recommend the Jesus Prayer as a means of turning the mind to God in meditation.

After you feel ready to move on from counting breaths, begin to say the Jesus Prayer without breaking the rhythm of your breathing. A series of ten or twenty such recitations of the Jesus Prayer will turn your mind to God, the object of your meditation and contemplation. The counting of breaths makes you present to yourself. The Jesus Prayer makes you present to God.

An explanation is necessary before I go on to the next step. We depend heavily on reason for knowledge, but reason can take us only so far. It's possible to know a thing directly by experiencing it. For example, a botanist knows a flower by studying each part in its roots, stem, leaves, and each of its flower parts, classifying them by shape, size, and color. A poet can see the same flower and know it by letting its beauty become a part of himself. The poet acquires a different kind of knowledge than the botanist's, but it is just as real. In knowing God, reason and words will take us only so far. At that point we abandon reason and rely on the poet's wordless kind of knowledge. The next practice is intended to lead to that goal. The Bible, especially the Gospels, is filled with sayings that are deceptively simple. We think we understand them when we read or hear them. But when we think about them we soon find that reason is altogether frustrated in piercing the shell of the words to reach the kernel of meaning. When reason, in thinking on these sayings, becomes stationary as the body is in its meditation position, then intuitive faculties take over and we stand wordless before God, awaiting the understanding only he can give.

With this as background we are ready for the next step of our meditation. Cease the concentration on the Jesus Prayer and propose to yourself these words of Jesus: "I am the vine, you are the branches. Whoever remains in me, with me in him, bears fruit in plenty; for cut off from me, you can do nothing." (John 15:5) You have heard these words countless times. Think about them. Even more, think about them prayerfully. In the course of your meditations on these words you may be moved to adoration, thanksgiving, contrition, or to petition. Do not repress these, for your meditation is a prayer, not the dry musings of a philosopher.

It is possible that this first saying might serve you as subject matter for two or even as many as five meditations. Do not use the materials that follow until you have exhausted the meaning of this first saying.

Even in this first meditation allow a few minutes of your time for wordless meditation. In this kind of prayer you are simply looking at God and being aware of his looking at you. In other words, you are present to God, who is beyond all your comprehension, unknowable in his true essence, and yet, because we have seen him in Jesus, lovable and full of love for us. Words will not encompass or explain him, so don't seek words. Just be in his presence with whatever fruits your meditation has given you.

When it is time to end your meditation, return to counting breaths, as explained before, for one or two series of ten. Follow this by saying the Jesus Prayer in rhythm with the breath for ten or fifteen breaths. Then let the body sway slightly from side to side, still repeating the prayer. Gradually enlarge the extent of this sway until you feel free. Then rise slowly.

Standing, place your right hand on your chest and cover it with your left hand. Begin to walk slowly, planting the heels firmly but gently upon the floor. Walk for a few minutes, keeping your mind fixed on the saying you were meditating on, or on the Jesus Prayer. After walking around for two or three minutes, slowly resume your daily tasks. Try keeping your meditation somewhere near your consciousness so that you carry it over into your day.

Summary

1. Assume one of the three positions, making sure that the spinal column is erect.

2. Begin with a deep breath, and release it silently through the nose.

3. Count breaths in series of ten.

4. Say the Jesus Prayer in rhythm to breathing.

5. Prayerfully meditate on the saying of Jesus.

6. Include a period of wordless prayer.

7. Conclude by again counting breaths, and

8. Saying the Jesus Prayer; then

9. Rouse the body from its inactivity.

10. Walk about meditatively for a few minutes before resuming your routine.

Second Meditation

After you've exhausted the saying for the first meditation, use the materials in this section. Do not spend more than five meditations on the first saying, for the insights you receive from meditating on the one that follows will illuminate the first one further. It's impossible to exhaust or totally comprehend the full meaning of these sayings through reason or intellect. If you persevere in meditation you will perhaps receive an enlightenment that surpasses intellectual comprehension. This is the gift of God and should be sought and received humbly.

Prepare for the second meditation by following the same steps as for the first, with this one exception. When you become present to yourself through counting breaths, count only on the completion of exhaling. Inhale, exhale, *one.* Inhale, exhale, *two.* And so on, up to ten, at which point begin again. This is a bit more difficult and forces you to a greater effort of concentration.

A word about distracting thoughts needs to be said here. Since your imagination is not being employed it will at times run wild. This is nothing to worry about and is quite natural. It is only after much meditation that you will acquire the ability to suppress the imagination to some degree. Right now, simply remain calm when you find you have been distracted, and renew your concentration. Check your posture, especially your back, when you are badly distracted. Soon you will find that you are concentrating even while images flit across your mind.

The second saying I recommend for meditation comes from St. Paul. "I live, now not I, but Christ lives in me." Propose this to yourself and consider it as before, not just intellectually, but prayerfully. Allow times of silence and wordless gazing at an unseen and ultimately unknowable God, for in these times of silence he speaks. As before, allow five or ten minutes of your meditation for this wordless gazing.

People often find that after about fifteen minutes they are tempted to conclude their meditation, and have felt that spending longer would be unprofitable. When they make an act of the will to continue they usually find that their concentration becomes deeper and their insights more penetrating. The first minutes of meditation are pleasant and the "work" does not seem burdensome. It won't become burdensome if, at an early moment of tiredness, you redouble your efforts.

Conclude the second meditation in the manner previously described. Again, when counting the breaths at the end of the meditation, count only on the exhaled breath. Proceed to the Jesus Prayer, and practice "walking meditation" for three to five minutes.

Meditate on this saying as long as you feel you are profiting from it. It may be for one meditation, or five. I would not recommend going beyond five on this one saying.

Succeeding Meditations

In your third meditation change your method of counting breaths once again — count only on the inhaling breath. This is the most difficult method of counting breaths and will help you to attain deeper concentration.

As for the sayings upon which you meditate, choose those that appeal to you from the New Testament, particularly the Gospels. Below are some suggestions. (Most of these are from the epistles because they continue the theme set out in the first two meditations. These are only suggestions and you may use your own selections.)

1. "For anyone who is in Christ, there is a new creation; the old creation is gone, and now the new one is here." (II Corinthians 5:17)

2. "God's love for us was revealed when God sent into the world his only Son, so that we may have life through him." (I John 4:9)

3. "If anyone acknowledges that Jesus is the Son of God, God lives in him and he in God." (I John 4:15)

4. "Anyone who has the Son has life; anyone who does not have the Son does not have life." (I John 5:12)

5. "The lamp of the body is the eye. It follows that if your eye is sound, your whole body will be filled with light. But if your eye is diseased, your whole body will be all darkness. If then, the light inside you is darkness, what darkness that will be!" (Matthew 6:22-23)

6. "Christ became obedient to death, even to death upon a cross. Therefore God exalted him and gave him a name above all names, so that at the name of Jesus all creatures on the earth, above and under the earth, should bend their knees and acknowledge that Jesus is Lord." (Philippians 2:8-11)

7. "We can know that we are living in him and he is living in us because he lets us share his Spirit." (I John 4:13)

8. "No one can say, 'Jesus is Lord,' unless he is under the influence of the Holy Spirit." (I Corinthians 12:3)

9. "The proof that you are sons is that God has sent the Spirit of his Son into our hearts: the Spirit that cries, 'Abba, Father.'" (Galatians 4:6)

10. "How happy are the poor in spirit. Theirs is the kingdom of heaven." (Matthew 5:3)

Concluding Observations

If you have persevered thus far you have found meditating an integral and enjoyable part of your daily life. No doubt you have also found that it has changed your life in many subtle ways. As you continue you will undoubtedly experience some difficulties which are useless to anticipate here. When you reach that point (and you'll know when you do) you will be fortunate if there is someone you can talk to and whose advice you can seek. A priest or a religious who is a faithful meditator will be a good guide at this point. If you can't find anyone rely on the advice of many good books available on prayer. Above all, look to the Bible, which by now should be your faithful companion. In it God speaks directly to us. Faithful reading of the Scriptures each day is the best preparation for meditation.

Books to Read

Most of these books are available in bookstores, or a public library.

Johnston, William.　*Christian Zen*
　　　　　　　　　The Still Point
　　　　　　　　　Silent Music
Graham, Aelred.　*Zen Catholicism*
Kapleau, Philip.　*The Three Pillars of Zen*
Merton, Thomas.　*Contemplative Prayer*
　　　　　　　　　Zen and the Birds of Appetite
Anonymous.　　　*The Cloud of Unknowing*
Anonymous.　　　*The Way of A Pilgrim*
　　　　　　　　　(On the Jesus Prayer)

Afterword

Meditation and contemplation should flow into liturgical prayer as well as into private vocal prayer and communal vocal prayer. These, in turn, enrich and flow back into meditation. Without meditation, however, no other form of prayer will be fully effective in our lives, not even liturgical prayer.

Since many people find their old forms of vocal prayer no longer meaningful, new forms are obviously needed. The second section makes suggestions for new forms of vocal prayer, private and communal.

SECTION TWO

NEW PRAYER FORMS

NEW PRAYER FORMS

Many persons who once found meaning and comfort in older forms of prayer now experience a sense of inadequacy in them. They have moved to a new understanding and relationship with God which the old forms no longer reflect. In such situations litanies, novenas, prayerbook ("cookbook") prayers, stations of the cross, and even the rosary seem false and hollow. This isn't because the old forms of prayer are false, but because they express a more meaningful reality to a particular person. Once God was totally the "other," entirely transcendent, and this has not necessarily changed. But God is also present in our world, living in our fellow humans and in the events of daily life. Perhaps now we are only beginning to make this presence of God real to ourselves as an operative force in our lives. This new and deepened vision of God requires that we find a way of relating to him what is true to us where we now stand. If our prayers are not true communications from the real us to the real God, they are not real prayers.

If you are comfortable with the old forms of prayer and find them an adequate expression of yourself to God, then by all means continue to use them. The following suggestions are meant for those who are seeking a new way to pray. For them I'll enumerate a number of prayer forms that others have used, and explain them as briefly as possible. The three sections will be A) private vocal prayer; B) communal vocal prayer; and C) life prayer forms.

A. PRIVATE VOCAL PRAYER

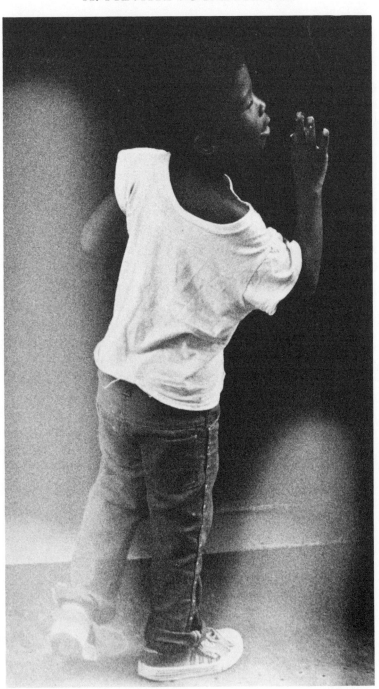

1. Singing

Singing hymns or some of the modern songs can be a form of prayer. There are songs that express our moods and speak to God about our present situation. Singing or humming such songs as we go about our daily rounds is a lifting of our minds and hearts to God. You might find the songs of Joseph Wise, Sebastian Temple, and Lucien Deiss popping into your head. These are good songs, expressing today's experience in today's idiom.

2. Pictures

Looking at pictures, especially religious pictures, whether in the Bible, on display, or as illustrations in magazines, can often lead directly to prayer. We see symbolism; or the expression on a face; or the position of a hand, and our emotions are touched, our understanding deepened. Prayer flows naturally. Meaningful pictures can be saved and compiled into a personal prayer book.

There are many posters and banners available today. The ones that speak to you can serve as a source of prayer. The pictures themselves predispose us to prayer. We need only train ourselves to take the next step — proceeding to prayer itself.

The use of pictures as the starting point and as a form of prayer is old and honorable. Whether we pray or not depends on how we approach pictures, statues, posters, and banners.

3. Reading

The reading of religious books, especially the Bible, can be a prayer. If you read slowly, stopping to think about a phrase and letting yourself talk about it with God, then reading becomes a prayer and will spill over into meditation. For many people this is the easiest and simplest form of prayer. It requires practice, however, for our natural tendency is to race through the material for intellectual content.

4. Repetition of a single prayer

Certain "formula" prayers have real meaning to some persons. For instance, repeating over and over the old prayer called the "Memorare" and the Prayer of St. Francis can be the deepest of prayers, each repetition seeing new depths, expressing the new understanding of the soul. If any "formula" prayer is dear to you, then it expresses your being and its repetition keeps you before God.

5. The Jesus Prayer

Dear to Russian spirituality is the Jesus Prayer, and whole spiritual lives have been built upon it. The Jesus Prayer is deceptively simple. Its form is, "Lord Jesus Christ, Son of God, have mercy on me, a sinner." Russian writers claim that the entire essence of the New Testament is contained in the prayer. They see a power in the name of Jesus itself.

To practice the Jesus Prayer, learn to say it in rhythm with your breathing. As you inhale, repeat silently, "Lord Jesus Christ, Son of God." As you exhale, repeat the second part of the prayer, "have mercy on me, a sinner." By assiduous practice you make this prayer automatic, so that it underlies all you do and say. In truth, you come to "pray always," "pray without ceasing." This Jesus Prayer passes beyond vocal prayer to meditation and contemplation if practiced long enough.

It would be an error to dismiss the Jesus Prayer lightly and without trial, for it has been a source of prayer at its deepest level to many in Russia, and indeed all over the world. For those who want to know more about it, a paperback book, *The Way of A Pilgrim*, by an anonymous Russian author, is readily available. It is interesting to note that is this prayer that serves as the final denouement of J. D. Salinger's *Franny and Zooey.*

6. Christian Mantra Praying

The mantra has become familiar to Western Christians through transcendental meditation and Hare Krishna people. The mantra is a sound symbol of the sacred, a phrase or sentence from sacred books. A short prayer, such as the Jesus Prayer, or phrases from Scriptures, such as "Jesus is Lord," or "My soul magnifies the Lord" may be chanted aloud for a period of time, say fifteen minutes or half an hour. This is a deceptively simple form of prayer and intellectual people might dismiss it as mindless repetition. It has depths, however, and you can try it to see if it is a prayer form that has meaning for you.

7. Repetition of a Single Word

The name of Jesus or the word "God" repeated slowly, with intervals, helps to focus the mind and serves as either a starting point for prayer or as a prayer in itself.

8. The Divine Office

The new breviary, *The Prayer of Christians*, easily found though expensive (about $13), is admirably designed as prayer. It is meant, as the title indicates, for all Christians, not only priests. Praying the morning, midday, or evening prayer is a wonderful custom. The time required is about fifteen minutes. A number of lay people are beginning to adopt this prayer which before was regarded the prerogative of the priest.

9. Dancing

There are some people who find dancing a prayer. Recently there has been a resurgence of liturgical dancing in many churches, including the Catholic Church. The movements of the body can express many of our deepest feelings and insights and can truly be a prayer. No doubt many people can really pray by dancing their message to God.

10. The Secret Name

Selecting a secret name can be a way of approaching God in an authentic manner. Select your name when you are taking a very close look at yourself. It will signify how you see yourself in relation to God. Perhaps you may call yourself "the Seeker," or even "the Sinner." Or your secret name might be a recurring failure in your life, such as "the Proud One." Perhaps a saint embodies an ideal which you wish to achieve. If you need to learn to love, you may be "Mary" or "the Magdalene." Or an animal may symbolize your nature: "the Bear," "the Lion." Whatever name you choose should have meaning to you and be as accurate as you can make it. When you approach God in prayer, present yourself to him under this name. "Lord," you pray, "here is the silly old sheep who so often gets lost, asking you to guide me to your pastures, for you are the Good Shepherd."

11. The Secret Color

Like the secret name, the secret color represents how you relate yourself to God, or how you wish to relate to him. A person in spiritual need might see himself as white, as an empty canvas awaiting God's brush strokes. A person conscious of guilt might see himself in the traditional black. A black person might choose that color because he wishes to approach God with all the special characteristics of his race. The chosen color is presented by the imagination as a background during times of prayer and recollection.

12. The Newspaper

The newspaper is the daily balance sheet of the world's work. It tells how the tasks of men are progressing. Since history is the unfolding of God's plan for the salvation and liberation of humankind, the daily paper contains many things to be prayed about. Hunger in distant places, threats of war, promises of peace, deaths and illnesses — all these have spiritual dimensions. Just as the Bible can be read meditatively, so can the newspaper. If we are aware of the extension of the daily news into eternity we can pause to praise, to thank, to adore, to make reparation.

13. The Secret Word

I am indebted to Sister Jean Hobday for this method of prayer. It is one she has used in teaching Indian children in Wyoming how to pray. At the beginning of the day you select a secret word, such as "give," "listen," "laugh," or "praise." Many times during the day you remind yourself of this word and try to live it.

14. *The Sacrifice Flower*

This too is a method used by Sister Jean Hobday. Pick a flower, such as a dandelion or a clover. Study it carefully, see its beauty, and let it remind you of God. Place it somewhere it will be often seen, and when it has withered bury it, since it gave its life to bring you a message of God.

15. Experiential Stations of the Cross

During Holy Week of 1973 I visited St. Clement's Church (Episcopal) in the theater district of New York. The pastor had invited people to use the church as a place of recollection and hermitage during this period, and some even lived there during the days of the Passion. In the far basement of the church someone had devised a modern stations of the cross. The first station, "Jesus is condemned to death," had these directions tacked to a post: "Cuss, swear, tear up a telephone book (provided), write the dirtiest words you know." Sure enough, a telephone book was there, and blackboard to write "the dirtiest words." Some of the dirty words that appeared there written by previous worshipers were "me," "sinner," "self." At the station, "Jesus carries his cross," a real cross was provided. I hoisted it to my shoulder where it dug in quite excruciatingly, and it seemed terribly heavy. A mattress on the floor provided a setting for "Jesus falls." Somehow the world has a different view when you are lying face-down. Perhaps somewhat dangerously a length of plastic was provided for the station "Jesus meets his mother." The directions were to wrap the plastic about the body and assume a fetal position. A simple pine box was provided for the station "Jesus dies on the cross," with the directions to lie down inside and close the lid, an invitation I forebore to accept.

All this sounds far out, yet praying through such stations of the cross was a moving experience. An individual or a group could easily think of their own stations, not necessarily fourteen in number, and provide experiences of the reality of the sufferings and death of Jesus.

I returned to St. Clement's for the Easter liturgy, joy-filled and alleluia-laden. At the lesson a Scripture was read first, and then short items from the newspaper, the last termed "a contemporary scripture." Then followed the Alleluia. People threw confetti and streamers while singing their Easter joy. The Easter liturgy was the perfect counterpoint to the stations of the cross.

B. COMMUNAL VOCAL PRAYER

1. Shared Prayer

A shared prayer group may be as few as two or as many as twenty or more. After a reading from Scripture participants pray and meditate silently until one wishes to share. The gift to the group may be a prayer expressed aloud in one's own words, or a reading from Scripture, or another source. Praying aloud in a group with no set formula may be difficult for some in the beginning. Since such groups usually meet once or twice a week the practice becomes normal. There is really nothing to say about shared prayer except to jump in and try it.

2. Charismatic, or Pentecostal Prayer

Charismatic prayer communities are found all over today. While it's possible this kind of prayer is not for you, the only way to find out is to attend several meetings of a group. Whether or not you persevere, this prayer has made a tremendous impact and has numerous adherents. Don't be put off by your initial impressions at first attendance at a group.

3. Scripture Services

There are many books of planned Scripture services and it is easy to devise your own. Scripture services may be held for an entire parish, a parish group, or a private group. The service consists of two or three Scripture readings on a theme, interspersed with set or spontaneous prayers.

4. Group Recitation of the Prayer of Christians

Two or more may pray together from the *Prayer of Christians*, mentioned above, alternating verses or strophes of the psalms. The book contains an explanation of group recitation.

Afterword on Communal Vocal Prayer

From my words on prayer in the introduction to this section it's obvious that religious congregations and communities should beware of trying to force one type of communal vocal prayer on its members. Communities should provide a variety of prayer forms from which the members may choose. It may be comforting to some to see a large number of people at their favorite prayer form, but harm can be done by dragooning individuals into situations that are meant to be prayer and a relationship with God.

Parishes should also provide a variety of prayer forms. The failure of most parishes to provide a variety of opportunities for individuals to pray together has been a source of impoverishment of the parishes. Individuals who wish to pray with others should strive to initiate suitable prayer forms into their own parishes.

C. GROUP MEDITATION

Though nothing is more individual than meditation a group may choose to meditate together for mutual encouragement and as a means of fulfilling the words of Jesus, "Where two or three are gathered together in my name, I am present in their midst." There are at least two places in New York City where Zen practitioners meet for meditation. Perhaps the day will come when there will be centers for Christian meditation, where people can come to meditate, receive instruction, and be advised. If any exist now I don't know of them.

Private meditation has the advantage of allowing people their own speed and individual development. On the other hand, there is support in meditating with others. The best groups are those that regularly pray and meditate together. A group consciousness and unity of purpose usually comes from this habitual common meditation. In some ways group meditation is more arduous than individual prayer, and for this reason the best introduction to meditation is praying alone. Group meditation is best when it is a supplement and an extension of individual meditation. Nor should groups be too large. Ten to fifteen is a good number, and perhaps twenty-five is the outermost acceptable number. If a group meets for instruction and prayer, then they can divide into smaller groups after the common portions of the gathering are completed.

When a group comes together to meditate each member should find a place to sit comfortably while a leader guides the efforts of the group. The meditation should not be longer than fifteen minutes. Each section of the meditation is read by the leader in a quiet, slow, reverential, and matter-of-fact voice, making pauses at the indicated places. A brief talk or a reading may precede the meditation, and a group sharing and evaluation follow it. Examples of group meditations follow.

A MEDITATION TO
UNDERSTAND ONE'S TRUE SELF

LEADER: Relax, but keep the back straight. Feel the feet relax; the ankles; the legs. Feel yourself sink into the chair. Relax your body, but keep the back straight. Relax the neck and face. Feel your mind relax. Breathe deeply and exhale quietly. Feel your relaxation increase as you count ten breaths, counting on each inhalation.

(Pause)

LEADER: Lord, my body is resting, but there is more to me than my body alone. I can make my body obey. My body serves you, Lord, and I wish to serve you with all my powers.

(Pause)

LEADER: Lord, my emotions often toss me about. Still, I am not my emotions. I can use them to serve you and my fellow dwellers on this earth, and not be ruled by my emotions. My emotions are nothing but an impetus to you.

(Pause)

LEADER: Lord, my mind is so often concerned only with my personal interests, and its wanderings often lead me down strange paths. Yet I am more than my mind alone. It is a beacon that points to you if only I will see.

(Pause)

LEADER: Lord, I feel my selfhood moving inside my body, my emotions, my mind. You have made me an individual, a person, a unique creation. I can follow myself only so far down into my being, and then I encounter a darkness where I can feel you present, though I cannot picture you or give you a name. Lord, I know that you are my life, and that my dependence on you is complete.

(*Pause*)

LEADER: Lord, I will share with others the life you have given me, even as I share their lives. My deeds will proclaim my union with you, and I will see you in the strengths and weaknesses of others. I, and everyone, meet you in each breath we take, in all we do. To be human is to discover our capacity for you.

(*Pause*)

LEADER: May God reveal himself to everyone in the depths of each personhood, and may all people show forth the love and glory of God. May he bless and keep us, let his light shine upon us, and give us peace.

(*Short Pause*)

LEADER: Let us close with a few quiet, easy breaths.

A HEALING MEDITATION

For physical, mental, or spiritual wounds.

LEADER: Relax, but keep the back straight. Feel the feet relax; the ankles; the legs. Feel yourself sink into the chair. Relax the body, but keep the back straight. Relax the neck and face. Feel your mind relax. Breathe deeply and let the breath come out quietly. Feel your relaxation increase as you count ten breaths, counting on each inhaling.

(Pause)

LEADER: Recall that you are always in God's presence. Go down deep into your selfhood, to where your selfhood and God's life in you are almost indistinguishable. Be conscious of God within you, and rest in his presence.

(Pause)

LEADER: Recall to your mind that which needs healing in you. Lay your need wordlessly before God, and be conscious of his strength and love. Respond wordlessly to his love and accept his strength.

(Pause)

LEADER: Let the strength of God make up for your weakness. Accept your weakness and acknowledge his strength and power.

(Pause)

LEADER: I thank you, Lord, for the strength you have given us. I will live in strength and accept my weakness. I give what I receive to others and to you.

(Pause)

LEADER: Let us close by breathing slowly, keeping our minds on God. With one breath let us rise in silence and confidence.

D. LIFE PRAYER FORMS

Some people are anxious to turn the very acts of daily life into prayer. If this is the only prayer, then it is suspect, for experience tells us that selfishness and self-considerations inevitably creep in. The saying, "work is prayer," has been criticized as self-deception. Indeed it well can be, for it is the common experience of those who try to build a life of prayer that work and other acts of daily life become prayerful only after long practice and much formal prayer. There is no denying, however, that our daily life should be a prayer, since Jesus is present in the events of our lives. Here, then, are some ways to experiment with this concept. At least you will become aware that all life may be a prayer.

1. Esthetic Experience

All beauty reflects God. The arts should appeal to what is highest and noblest in our nature. Music, painting, sculpture, dance and drama can all speak to us of our relations with each other and with God. If we open ourselves to the spiritual dimensions of esthetic experiences they can become a prayer. The same thing can be said of the beauty of nature, or the beauty of the human face, and natural gracefulness. Athletics, "the people's ballet," can speak to us of the possibilities God has given us. Everything, it we attune ourselves, can speak to us of God and serve as a medium for his message to us.

2. Daily Work

Our work can speak to us of God the Creator and the God who cares for his people. The farmer, the baker, the grocer can apply to themselves the words of Jesus, "I was hungry, and you gave me food to eat." Each job serves people in some way, and to serve our fellow humans is to serve Jesus himself. If we are aware of our intention to serve people as we work and are not merely intent on making money, our work can become a prayer. This is a tricky area, full of possibilities for self-deception. Work can be, and should be, a prayer, but it should never be our only prayer.

3. Interpersonal Relationships

Jesus makes no distinction between himself and his members. What we do to them we do to him. If we are aware of the "Christness" of the people with whom we live, speak, and interact, we are praying. We give and receive God among ourselves.

4. Seeking the Will of God

Each day we have to make innumerable decisions, small and great. If in each of these turning points we seek the will of God and learn to make decisions with his help and in the light of his message, we are living prayerfully. Many things also occur without our decision. In these we can become aware of God working in our life, conscious of his presence shaping us as we experience life.

A CONCLUDING WORD ON PRAYER

Prayer is the gift of God, for, as St. Paul says, "No one can say 'Jesus is Lord' unless he is under the influence of the Holy Spirit." (I Corinthians 12:3) Your director in prayer, then, is none other than the Spirit that worked in Jesus. Formulas and methods may be helpful places to start, but in all things yield yourself to the Holy Spirit who will teach you to pray.

Liturgical prayer is without doubt the highest form of prayer, for in it Jesus himself prays and permits us to add our voices. No one who neglects liturgical prayer can claim to have a prayer life of any sort. The golfer who thinks he finds God on the course on Sunday is deluding himself. Likewise, communal vocal prayer is a higher form of prayer than private vocal prayer, for Jesus promised he would be a member of a group that met to pray. In spite of the pre-eminence of liturgical and communal prayer, it is meditation that has the greatest potential for placing us in a personal relationship with God. It is meditation that can help us make a change in our understanding and values. It is meditation that integrates all the phases of our life, natural and supernatural. For these reasons I cannot stress too much the necessity of meditation for a deep spiritual life.

Prayer is nothing less than a personal relationship with God. Like all relationships it grows and deepens and becomes habitual. One who has prayed for a long time, especially in meditation, finds that mature prayer is much different from beginning prayer. It's necessary to be willing to change as we mature in prayer, not to cling to old forms and manners of praying. The Holy Spirit is our guide, and if we keep our eyes on him, he will lead us smoothly up each step of our growing relationship with God.

In this relationship with God it is he who takes the initiative, and for that reason there is nothing that can be said with absolute dogmatism about prayer. It follows then, that everything that has been written here is nothing more than a rough guide. It was intended as a help. The real helper, and the real end, is God.

NOTES